The Life and Adventures of a Dog named Sweety

Doreen D. Diana

The Life and Adventures of a Dog named Sweety

iUniverse books may be ordered through booksellers or by contacting:

iUniverse
1663 Liberty Drive
Bloomington, IN 47403
www.iuniverse.com
1-800-Authors (1-800-288-4677)

ISBN: 978-1-5320-7887-3 (sc)
ISBN: 978-1-5320-7888-0 (hc)
ISBN: 978-1-5320-7889-7 (e)

Library of Congress Control Number: 2019910909

Print information available on the last page.

iUniverse rev. date: 08/16/2019

Contents

Preface

My book tells a few stories about a female pit bull terrier who is adopted, touching on the challenges a pet and pet owner might come across, along with a few amazing chapters.

Pit bulls seem to get a bad name, but I believe the way a dog is raised determines his or her actions. All animals will try to defend themselves if they feel threatened.

Each chapter has a moral, and I've included a few activities at the end of the book. You can also meet Sweety live (further information is located at the back of the book).

Some pictures in the book were drawn or taken to depict the actual areas involved. If you enjoy this book, watch for book 2, in which Sweety loses her privileges, gets skunked, and more. Thank you!

Chapter 1
The Adoption

The day, I would adopt Sweety, the female pit bull terrier, had come. I arrived at the animal shelter. There were many different animals up for adoption at the shelter. I saw cats, bunny rabbits, and dogs.

I went to the back of the shelter to look for Sweety. I had seen her a few times before, and she seemed friendly and quiet and allowed me to pet her.

There were lots of dogs waiting to be adopted. Most of them were pit bulls. I took the identification card on Sweety's cage. The card had her name on it, along with other information to identify her.

When I brought the card up to the front desk, the workers had to do a background check on me. They did this to be sure I was a qualified pet owner for Sweety.

At animal shelters, the staff want the animals to find good homes for the long term. They want to be sure the animals are not placed in a home only to be brought to another home or back to the shelter again. This can be hard on an animal.

After the background check, the staff went to get Sweety and brought her to the front desk area. They took Sweety into a room and gave her a few shots to prevent illness.

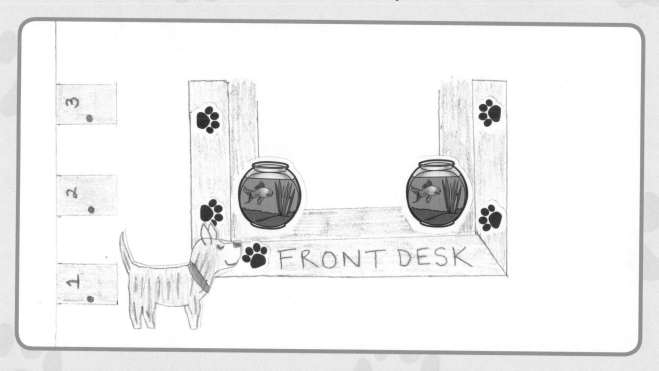

She also got a chip placed in her, in case she ever got lost. Sweety didn't mind. She was getting a new home. I finished up the paperwork, and the staff put Sweety's leash on her and handed the leash to me.

I brought Sweety outside and allowed her to go to the bathroom. Then I brought her to the car. Sweety was afraid to get in the car and needed lots of encouragement, but she finally got in the car. Then we were on our way home.

Remember to pick up after your pet and keep your community clean.

Chapter 2
Patience and Time

When I arrived at Sweety's new home, she was a little scared. I told her it was okay and brought her into my home.

I took the leash off and showed her each room in the house. She ran up and down the stairs. When we got to the basement stairs, Sweety went down the stairs but was afraid to come back up the stairs, so I carried her up the stairs.

Those stairs were different. They had an open space between each step, and Sweety was afraid she would fall through.

Finally, she got used to the steps and went up and down on her own.

Sweety got excited, and she had an accident on the floor. I put the leash on Sweety, brought her outside, and explained to her, "This is where you go potty."

It took a couple of weeks to get Sweety housebroken. I tried taking her out every two hours to go to the bathroom. I also took her out every morning when I first got up and every night before I went to bed.

This worked out well, and Sweety no longer had accidents in the house. Sweety learned to bark to let me know she needed to go to the bathroom.

Remember to take time and have patience when caring for a new pet.

Chapter 3

Boundaries and Personal Space

It was a special day for Sweety. Before Sweety came to my home, there was a wild rabbit that would come around. I named the rabbit, Bunny. Bunny would come to my house and eat berries and plants in my yard. Now I had to let Bunny know a dog lived there.

One day Bunny was outside in the yard, and I went out and talked to Bunny, saying, "Sweety lives here now, and she has a leash that goes up to the big tree." I pointed to the big tree. I told Bunny, "Do not go past the tree when Sweety is outside." Bunny looked at me and then kept eating.

I also talked to Sweety, telling her that Bunny came around there to eat. I put Sweety on her leash, and then Bunny showed up. Sweety started barking, but Bunny didn't care because Bunny knew that Sweety was tied up.

Every day when Sweety went outside, she looked for Bunny. Bunny showed up every so often. One day Bunny brought another rabbit to the house, and they both ran around the backyard. Sweety was on her leash, just watching them.

Bunny was smart. One day Sweety was tied up in the front yard, and Bunny came by. Bunny knew Sweety was on her leash and could go only so far, so Bunny sat about five feet away from Sweety and ate. Sweety just barked.

It is important to set boundaries and give personal space when needed.

Chapter 4
Shelter

When Sweety woke up one morning, it was raining outside. I put Sweety on her leash so she could go to the bathroom. I told her to hurry up so she wouldn't get too wet.

I saw Sweety looking at a bush and noticed that Bunny was there. Bunny was under the bush, staying out of the rain.

I explained to Sweety that all animals needed shelter. I was not sure if she understood me. She just stared at me and then at Bunny.

When Sweety came back into the house, she left paw prints on the kitchen floor. Then I had to mop the floor. Sweety did not like to stay out in the rain for long. For the rest of the day, Sweety just lay around.

Remember that all living things need some type of shelter at times.

Chapter 5

Friendship

It was going to be another special day for Sweety. Sweety was going to meet my brother for the first time. You see, my brother was going to dog-sit for me while I went on vacation.

I had never been away from Sweety for any length of time. I wanted Sweety to be comfortable and stay at home instead of going to a kennel.

When my brother arrived, Sweety was excited. She began wagging her tail and jumped on my brother to say hello. Usually, if I told Sweety to get down, she would listen to me.

I showed my brother where all Sweety's things were kept, including toys I'd bought her to keep her busy. Sweety saw me packing my suitcase, so she knew I was going away.

While I was on vacation, I called home a couple of times to check on things. My brother said Sweety was doing well and slept near him at night.

Sweety enjoyed having company and building a friendship with my brother. When I talked to Sweety on the phone, her ears would go up, and then she would look around for me.

It is important to build positive friendships throughout life.

Chapter 6
Bullying

One day Sweety was going to the dog park. The dog park had different areas to keep the big dogs with big dogs and the little dogs with little dogs. Sweety got to go play with the big dogs.

Sweety had been to the dog park before. At the dog park, a pet had to be on a leash until the owner got through the gate. Then the owner could take the leash off. So that was what we did.

Sweety got excited and ran to the other dogs. She tended to follow them around and then went off on her own. Well, that day, there were quite a few dogs, and they were of different breeds.

One dog kept bothering some of the others dogs. Sweety just ignored that dog. Then two other dogs came into the dog park area, and the dog that was bothering the other dogs started to growl at the two new dogs.

The two new dogs were not going to put up with the bullying, and they began to fight back. Sweety saw this going on and tried to get in the middle of it. It seemed Sweety was trying to break up the fight. I put Sweety on her leash and took her home.

If someone is bullying you or anyone else around you, walk away, and tell somebody. No one should be bullied.

Chapter 7
The Rescue

It was an eventful day for Sweety. I let her out of the house in the morning so she could go to the bathroom. The next thing I knew, I heard Sweety barking and barking.

I decided to go outside to see what she was barking at. When I reached Sweety, I noticed an orange-and-white kitten with its head in an empty can of dog food. I was a little scared because I didn't know if the kitten was still alive.

I moved the can of dog food with my foot, and the kitten backed its head out of the can and ran up a tree. I was happy to see the kitten was alive, but now I had another problem: the kitten was stuck up in the tree. I put Sweety in the house and grabbed a ladder. The ladder was too short, and I couldn't reach the kitten. I could tell the kitten was scared.

I called 911, and they put me through to the local fire department. A firefighter came to my house in a little fire truck. I explained the situation, and he said, "A big fire truck is on the way."

The fire truck pulled down the alley behind my house, and two firefighters got out of the truck. They grabbed a big ladder and walked toward us. The kitten kept looking at me, then at the firefighters, and then at me again.

The kitten then decided to jump from the tree into my arms and then to the ground. The kitten then ran through a gap in the fence into the neighbors' yard. The firefighters and I just chuckled. The firefighters put the ladder away and headed back to the firehouse.

Be kind to all.

Glossary

adoption: The act of taking something on as your own, (for example, Sweety is now a part of my family).

background check: The history of a person's experience, related to certain situations.

boundary: Something that indicates a limit (for example, Sweety could only go so far on her leash).

bullying: Mistreatment of another by one who feels more powerful (for example, the dog at the dog park).

community: A group of people living in a particular area.

encouragement: An attempt to persuade or inspire with courage.

long term: Occurring over a long period of time.

patience: Being calm in certain situations without complaining.

personal space: The distance at which one feels comfortable when talking to or being next to another person.

qualified: Fit for a given purpose or able to take on a new role.

shelter: Something that covers or gives protection, (for example, Bunny under the bush, getting out of the rain).

Questions for thought

How do you feel about adopting a pet?

Would you adopt a young pet that is very active? If so, why?

Would you adopt an older pet that is calm and relaxed? If so, why?

Would you have the time and patience involved with owning a new pet?

What would you do if your pet was at the dog park and a dogfight had started? This does not happen often, but it could.

Will you remember to clean up after your pet, while taking the pet for a walk around your neighborhood or community?

Do you have a plan to take care of your pet when you will not be home for an extended period of time?

These are just questions for discussion if and when the time comes, that a child may ask for a pet.

C	O	M	M	U	N	I	T	Y	S	B	B
Q	H	R	A	I	N	Y	D	A	Y	U	A
A	U	E	D	Z	J	C	V	K	R	L	S
D	L	T	C	B	A	A	P	I	K	L	E
O	S	H	B	U	N	N	Y	T	D	Y	M
P	A	G	F	S	I	R	B	T	T	I	E
T	K	I	D	H	M	Z	F	E	R	N	N
I	I	F	O	Y	A	G	E	N	E	G	T
O	N	E	G	Q	L	W	S	B	E	P	C
N	D	R	P	B	S	T	A	I	R	S	K
Y	N	I	A	R	H	R	E	S	C	U	E
A	E	F	R	I	E	N	D	S	H	I	P
D	S	P	K	C	L	A	D	D	E	R	G
Y	S	A	P	A	T	I	E	N	C	E	T
N	I	W	O	I	E	L	I	F	E	U	I
N	Y	R	M	G	R	A	B	B	I	T	S
U	X	E	T	K	B	S	D	A	P	H	G
B	O	U	N	D	A	R	I	E	S	W	O
M	W	F	I	R	E	T	R	U	C	K	D
A	D	V	E	N	T	U	R	E	S	I	T

ADOPTION FIREFIGHTER STAIRS
ADVENTURES FIRE TRUCK SWEETY
ANIMAL SHELTER FRIENDSHIP TIME
BASEMENT KINDNESS TREE
BOUNDARIES KITTEN
BULLYING LADDER
BUNNY LIFE
BUSH PATIENCE
CAN PAW
COMMUNITY RABBITS
DOG PARK RAINY DAY
DOG SIT RESCUE

```
C O M M U N I T Y S B B
Q H R A I N Y D A Y U A
A U E D Z J C V K R L S
D L T C B A N P I K L E
O S H B U N Y B T D Y M
P A G F S I R B T T I E
T K I D H M Z F E R N N
I I F O Y A G E E E G T
O N E G Q L W S B E P C
N D R P B S T A I R S K
Y E A I H R E S C U E E
A S P R E N D S D E I P
D S A C L I E N C E R T
Y I W A T L I F E C E I
N Y O P R A B B I T U S
U X M G B S D A P H G G
B O U N D A R I E S W O
M W F I R E T R U C K D
A D V E N T U R E S I T
```

ADOPTION	FIREFIGHTER	STAIRS
ADVENTURES	FIRE TRUCK	SWEETY
ANIMAL SHELTER	FRIENDSHIP	TIME
BASEMENT	KINDNESS	TREE
BOUNDARIES	KITTEN	
BULLYING	LADDER	
BUNNY	LIFE	
BUSH	PATIENCE	
CAN	PAW	
COMMUNITY	RABBITS	
DOG PARK	RAINY DAY	
DOG SIT	RESCUE	

34

Can you find 9 things that are different?

Printed in the United States
By Bookmasters